RESIDENT ALIEN

Stuart Spencer

BROADWAY PLAY PUBLISHING INC
224 E 62nd St, NY, NY 10065
www.broadwayplaypub.com
info@broadwayplaypub.com

RESIDENT ALIEN
© Copyright 2004 by Stuart Spencer

First printing: May 2004
I S B N: 0-88145-241-6

Book design: Marie Donovan
Word processing: Microsoft Word
Typographic controls: Xerox Ventura Publisher 2.0 P E
Typeface: Palatino
Printed and bound in the U S A

ORIGINAL PRODUCTION

RESIDENT ALIEN was first produced by the Actors
Theater of Louisville as part of the 22nd Annual
Humana Festival of New American Plays, opening
on 24 February 1998. The cast and creative contributors
were:

MICHAEL .... William McNulty
PRISCILLA .... Carolyn Swift
RAY .... Brad Bellamy
THE ALIEN .... V Craig Heidenreich
THE SHERIFF .... Brian Keeler
BILLY .... Corey Thomas Logsdon

Director .... Judy Minor
Scenic design .... Paul Owen
Costume design .... Nanzi Adzima
Lighting design .... Amy Appleyard
Sound design .... Martin R Desjardins
Properties design .... Ron Riall
Stage manager .... Juliet Horn
Assistant stage manager .... Charles M Turner III
Dramaturg .... Michael Bigelow Dixon
Casting .... Laura Richin Casting

CHARACTERS & SETTING

MICHAEL
PRISCILLA
RAY
THE ALIEN
THE SHERIFF
BILLY

All the characters are in their thirties, except BILLY,
who is about twelve.

*The stage setting should be minimal, fluid enough that the
scenes can change easily and quickly.*

ACT ONE

Scene One

(A farmhouse in Wisconsin. Late at night)

(On stage are MICHAEL *and* PRISCILLA *and* RAY. MICHAEL *sits in a chair.* PRISCILLA *and* RAY *circle around him.)*

MICHAEL: He wanted to go to the quarry. I said,
"No, Billy, it's too close to bedtime." He said,
"Come on, Dad. I want to see the sunset. It's summer.
I don't have to get up for school."
  So I said, "Fine. But don't tell your mother."
  So we're walking through the woods, and it's already
dark in there, even though the sky is still blue. And we
get to that clearing—you know, where the trail heads
off to the left there? And there was this light. Above,
and behind us. Then it started to move towards
us—this light—and we ran back down the trail,
but it followed us.
  Then we saw it, right in front of us, on the ground.
The light changed color and focused, like a narrow
beam, pointing right at Billy. And Billy walked towards
it, like a trance. But I was frozen in place. I couldn't
move! And I yelled, "No! Take me! Take me!"
  And then...it was gone. One second, it was there.
The next...nothing. And I was alone.
  At least I thought I was alone. They left someone.
One of their own. He said, "We borrowed your friend.
Don't worry. He'll be fine."

(PRISCILLA *walks up to him, confronting him.*)

PRISCILLA: Bullshit.

RAY: Okay, okay! Now hold on here. Okay Mike, so—that's all just fine. So, where is he now?

MICHAEL: I just told you, he's in the ship.

RAY: Not Billy—this guy they left. This alien.

PRISCILLA: Why are you asking him that?!

RAY: Because maybe we could talk to him.

PRISCILLA: Ray, there is no little green man.

RAY: Let's just hear the guy out once. Okay Mike, if they left someone, then where is he?

MICHAEL: I...I don't know. He left. He's not here.

RAY: He left? Where did he go?

MICHAEL: He didn't say. He said not to look for him.

RAY: And you didn't, I suppose.

MICHAEL: I'm not going to do anything he said not to. They have Billy.

RAY: But if he knows where Billy is ...

MICHAEL: He's in a spaceship!

PRISCILLA: Fine. We're calling the sheriff.

MICHAEL: Go ahead. Call the sheriff. It's not going to do any good.

RAY: (*To* PRISCILLA) He's right about that. If it's aliens, there's not much Hank's going to be able to do.

PRISCILLA: Ray.

MICHAEL: They took him away and he's not coming back until they decide.

PRISCILLA: Michael, you have bullshitted me once too often // and you're not going to do it again...

MICHAEL: *(Overlapping at //)* Bullshat.

PRISCILLA: What?!

MICHAEL: "Bullshat" would be correct.

PRISCILLA: *(To RAY, suddenly at a loss)* You see what I'm dealing with?!

MICHAEL: You're a literate woman, Priscilla. I don't know why you pretend you're not.

PRISCILLA: You are not dragging me into a fight about the past tense of shit. No! I'm sorry! I refuse!

RAY: All right now Mike. Come on here. You don't expect us to really believe this.

MICHAEL: It's not a question of believing. When something happens to you—when it happens present tense, first person—then it's not like you either believe or you don't believe. It's just a matter of what happened to you. If you're in a car accident and you break your left arm, you don't go around afterwards saying, "Now I believe in car accidents." You just say, "I was in an accident. That's what happened to me."

PRISCILLA: You have a history, you know. It wouldn't be the first time you made things up, invented stories, imagined things that aren't true.

MICHAEL: I never "imagined" things!

PRISCILLA: You displayed an inability to distinguish between reality and fantasy! The shrink said that, not me!

MICHAEL: I was there! I saw it!

PRISCILLA: Oh yes, you always concocted stories, Michael, but at least it was always something original!

MICHAEL: Priscilla, this happened!

PRISCILLA: I'll take you into court if I have to.

MICHAEL: You do what you have to do. You always did.

PRISCILLA: You've taken advantage of my good nature too many times, Michael! I am Billy's legal custodian. Your visitation rights are all spelled out.

MICHAEL: I can't help what the people in spaceships do!

RAY: Okay, okay. Listen you two. It's time to saw this off. I got to get up and go fishing early.

PRISCILLA: You're not going fishing, mister.

RAY: I told Roger I was going to meet him up at Machickanee Flowage.

PRISCILLA: *(To* MICHAEL*)* If my son isn't on my doorstep first thing tomorrow morning, I'm calling the sheriff's office and I'm going to have you arrested. Is that clear? So you'd better go back out to the quarry, stick out your thumb, flag down that spaceship, and get them to beam Billy back down to earth before his mother throws one hell of an interplanetary fit. *(She exits.)*

MICHAEL: They don't beam people. That's T V.

RAY: See if you can't bring the kid back quick this time, eh Mike? They're really bitin' up to the Flowage. *(He exits.)*

(The door to the laundry opens and THE ALIEN *enters. He has a slightly greenish tinge to his skin.)*

ALIEN: Which one were you married to?

(Lights out.)

Scene Two

(The same, somewhat later, still night. MICHAEL *has fallen asleep, his head on the table. The* ALIEN *sits at the table, struggling with a book.* MICHAEL *wakes up with a start.)*

ALIEN: Hi.

MICHAEL: You're really here.

ALIEN: Yes.

MICHAEL: I thought maybe I was just dreaming.

(He rubs his eyes and checks his watch. He was sleeping longer than he thought.)

ALIEN: Sleep must be very boring.

MICHAEL: Actually it can be quite interesting.

ALIEN: Pretty slow going from this end. You do it a lot?

MICHAEL: Every night.

ALIEN: Wow. Sure wish you had a T V.

MICHAEL: Well I don't. I threw it out.

ALIEN: Bummer.

MICHAEL: *(Referring to the book)* What're you reading?

ALIEN: It's yours. Kierkegaard. I hope you don't mind.

MICHAEL: How do you like it?

ALIEN: I'm still working on the first sentence, actually. *(He reads.)* "If there were no eternal consciousness in a man, if at the bottom of everything there were only a wild ferment, a power that twisting in dark passions produced everything great or inconsequential; if an unfathomable, insatiable emptiness lay hid beneath everything, what would life be but despair?"
Now what does that mean, exactly?

MICHAEL: It means there has to be something else.

ALIEN: Expand.

MICHAEL: Something other than mere passion, mere animalistic drive. Life is not only the wolf howling at the moon without consciousness. Life has meaning. Humanity has thought. We are aware, we're sentient. We endow the world with meaning through thought. We try to understand the nature of our own howl.

ALIEN: I see. *(He closes the book and hands it to* MICHAEL.*)* I guess I like more of a story.

MICHAEL: *(He takes the book and goes to the window.)* It's almost daylight.

ALIEN: Yes.

MICHAEL: They'll be back soon.

ALIEN: They will?

MICHAEL: You said they'd be back this morning.

ALIEN: Did I?

MICHAEL: Wait a minute. They won't be back this morning? Billy's not on his way home?

ALIEN: I'm sorry if you misunderstood // but I...

MICHAEL: *(Overlapping at //)* Nobody misunderstood! You said they'd be back by sunrise!

ALIEN: I said "they always come back by sunrise". I didn't say this particular sunrise?

MICHAEL: I trusted you!

ALIEN: Don't worry. It's all for a good cause. And they'd never hurt a soul.

MICHAEL: How do I know that?

ALIEN: How do you know he's not having a great time up there? He might be.

MICHAEL: Well, how much longer?

ALIEN: I don't know.

MICHAEL: Are we talking days? Weeks? Months? What?!

ALIEN: Oh days, days. At the very most, a week. Or two.

MICHAEL: Just tell me the truth. This is my son we're talking about!

ALIEN: Well I don't know. That's the truth. Sometimes it's short, sometimes it's long. But they always put the people back where they came from.

MICHAEL: Always?

ALIEN: Always.

MICHAEL: Really?

ALIEN: Almost certainly.

MICHAEL: I'm going back to the clearing.

ALIEN: Please don't do that.

MICHAEL: Why shouldn't I?

ALIEN: I worry about you.

MICHAEL: I can take care of myself.

ALIEN: You're upset. When people are upset they do things they don't mean to do.

MICHAEL: How would you know? What do you know about people? You said you'd never seen any people before me.

ALIEN: I said I never saw any humans. People I've seen all over the galaxy.

MICHAEL: Well, I am a people and I have to find my son.

ALIEN: I know, but believe me, he's not at the clearing. Not even close. Now please, won't you sit down?

(MICHAEL *resists for a moment, but finally gives in.*)

ALIEN: Here. Drink your coffee.

(MICHAEL *stares into his coffee.*)

MICHAEL: It's cold.

ALIEN: You don't like cold coffee?

MICHAEL: No.

ALIEN: Boy, things sure are different down here.
See, to wake up in the morning we drink martinis—
steaming hot. But we drink our coffee cold, at night,
when we want to party up.

MICHAEL: Down.

ALIEN: What?

MICHAEL: I think you mean party down.

ALIEN: You see? Cultural exchange. I love it! Mind if I
smoke? *(He takes out cigarettes and lights one.)* Smoking
helps control our libido.

MICHAEL: What's wrong with your libido?

ALIEN: Nothing wrong with it. It's incredibly high,
that's all. Wait a second, I forgot—you like to
distinguish between gender here, don't you.

MICHAEL: Well, yes.

ALIEN: See, we don't do that.

MICHAEL: You sleep with anyone?

ALIEN: Not anyone. But somebody attractive,
like yourself...

(MICHAEL *flashes him a worried look.*)

ALIEN: Relax, I'm smoking. It's fine.

MICHAEL: Could you just tell me one thing?

ALIEN: Of course.

MICHAEL: Why did you take him?

ALIEN: We prefer the term 'borrow'.

MICHAEL: Oh right. I feel so secure about my only
son when you say you only "borrowed" him.
My compliments to your language experts.
They must be up on their George Orwell.

ALIEN: George Orwell. *1984*. Good movie.

MICHAEL: It's also a book.

ALIEN: Yeah, but once you see the movie, it sort of
spoils it.

MICHAEL: The question is: why?

ALIEN: I think I lost you.

MICHAEL: Why did you take him?

ALIEN: Borrow.

MICHAEL: Why?

ALIEN: Some obscure test to investigate some statistical
aberration in some previous test that is part of some
longer, on-going survey that's part of some endless
study of some tiny little behavioral quirk. You know
what these people are like: inquisitive, eager little
minds. So annoying.

MICHAEL: Billy's not in any danger, is he?

ALIEN: Well that's a relative question. No pun intended.

(MICHAEL *doesn't crack a smile.*)

ALIEN: See, you're his relative and...never mind.

MICHAEL: Is he in danger?

ALIEN: Let me put it this way. He walks to school
everyday, right?

MICHAEL: Yes.

ALIEN: Is that dangerous?

MICHAEL: Of course not.

ALIEN: Well, but—getting hit by an automobile or accosted by some random lunatic. You never know.

MICHAEL: Well there's some danger just in getting up in the morning.

ALIEN: There you go. Couldn't say it any better.

MICHAEL: You don't even know what's going on up there, do you.

ALIEN: Hey, I'm support team, okay? It's some kind of very fancy I Q test. I don't know the details.

MICHAEL: I thought you were an advanced race.

ALIEN: Advanced race, yes. But I work in the kitchen. I'm a...what's your word again? Carboy?

MICHAEL: Busboy.

ALIEN: Right...

MICHAEL: If you're a busboy, then what are you doing here?

ALIEN: Shore leave.

MICHAEL: This is insane.

ALIEN: Look, it's been a long time stacking plates and filling water glasses, okay? I need a break. And from everything I hear, earth sounds like a pretty good time. Best T V shows, best C Ds, best magazines, best movies, best snacks. Best everything! I was hoping you could give me a sort of a tour—I'd love to do an outlet mall, for instance.

MICHAEL: Is this common? "Shore leave"?

ALIEN: No—strictly forbidden. They'd kill me if they found out.

MICHAEL: Kill you?!

ALIEN: Well, no. But they might make me scrub pots all the way to the next solar system.

MICHAEL: So you know nothing.

ALIEN: No.

MICHAEL: You're useless.

ALIEN: I think I have a few skills.

MICHAEL: But essentially, you're useless. My boy is kidnapped and....

ALIEN: Borrowed.

MICHAEL: My boy is kidnapped, and you're just here to "party up".

ALIEN: Down.

MICHAEL: I know.

ALIEN: Listen, I could have just walked off and left you back at the clearing, but I happen to be warmhearted by nature.

MICHAEL: I don't want a warm-hearted alien mall rat! I want my son!

ALIEN: How would you have like it if I just walked out right now?

MICHAEL: Better than this!

ALIEN: You don't mean that.

MICHAEL: Oh yes, I do.

(THE ALIEN *stamps out his cigarette.*)

ALIEN: Okay. Have it your way. We'll see how you like it when I'm not around.

MICHAEL: Where are you going?

ALIEN: Out.

MICHAEL: There's no where to go. It's five am.
Everything's closed.

ALIEN: That's all right. I can wait. Maybe I'll find
somebody who's grateful to have me around.

MICHAEL: But what if I need you? Where are you going?

ALIEN: To find myself a good time! *Ciao*, baby!

(THE ALIEN *takes a swig of coffee, gasps at the punch it
packs, and exits.* MICHAEL *stares after him.*)

(Lights out.)

Scene Three

(The same. The next morning. 8:30)

(THE SHERIFF *waits while* MICHAEL *is dressing for work.
He listens to the radio playing the triumphant, joyous end
of the First Movement of Beethoven's* Seventh Symphony.
It sounds tinny and thin on the radio.)

(The music pauses for a moment.)

SHERIFF: I just stopped by to....

(The music continues, then finishes.)

SHERIFF: I just stopped by to...

MICHAEL: Shh!

RADIO ANNOUNCER: That was Beethoven's Seventh
Symphony, conducted by // Herbert von Karajan of
the Berlin Philharmonic...

MICHAEL: *(Overlapping at //)* What?!

SHERIFF: What's wrong?

MICHAEL: God, I hate it when they do that. I give those
guys money.

SHERIFF: What did they do?

MICHAEL: There's another three movements for cryin' out loud! *(To the radio)* Play the whole damn symphony or don't play it at all! *(He flicks off the radio.)* And you could knock.

SHERIFF: *(Forced cheerfulness)* 'morning.

(MICHAEL starts to put on his K-Mart uniform.)

(THE SHERIFF notices the Kierkegaard on the table. He fingers it.)

SHERIFF: *Fear and Trembling.* Soren...

MICHAEL: Kierkegaard.

SHERIFF: Any good?

MICHAEL: It's a page turner. What time is it?

SHERIFF: Time for some of that good coffee you make.

MICHAEL: It's all gone. Can I please have the time?

SHERIFF: What's the matter, lose your watch?

MICHAEL: I threw out my watch—it only reminded I'm always late.

SHERIFF: It's 8:28.

MICHAEL: I'm late.

SHERIFF: Well, Priscilla called about some sort of problem with Billy.

MICHAEL: Yeah, there's a problem. He's in a spaceship at the moment. As soon as he's back on earth, I'll send him right over. I promise.

SHERIFF: Now, Michael—Billy is her child too. This is no way to deal with...whatever.

MICHAEL: Why can't you just try to believe me, Hank?

SHERIFF: We'd just like to know where Billy is.

MICHAEL: I told you where he is.

SHERIFF: In a spaceship.

MICHAEL: Yes.

SHERIFF: Is there a phone in this spaceship? So maybe we could talk to Billy?

MICHAEL: You know, I'm just guessing—but I bet there isn't.

SHERIFF: Well, a radio then. Some sort of communication device. *(He flips his hand open a la* Star Trek*)* You know—"Kirk to Enterprise." That kind of thing. So we make sure Billy's okay. It'd take a load off Priscilla's mind, I can tell you.

MICHAEL: If there was some way to talk to Billy, don't you think I would have done it?

SHERIFF: So you haven't talked to him.

MICHAEL: No!

SHERIFF: And you're not planning on it in the near future.

MICHAEL: If I could I would, and I can't!

SHERIFF: All right, okay. Just a thought.

MICHAEL: Look, do you mind? You don't keep K-Mart waiting if you know what's good for you.

SHERIFF: Well, I've got a couple more questions.

*(*MICHAEL *gestures impatiently for him to continue.)*

SHERIFF: Priscilla said you mentioned someone else.

MICHAEL: He's not here.

SHERIFF: So there was another person with you.

MICHAEL: It's one of them. An alien.

SHERIFF: I see.

MICHAEL: On the ship he's actually just a busboy.

SHERIFF: What's he doing down here?

MICHAEL: Taking some unauthorized shore leave. He's AWOL.

SHERIFF: An AWOL alien busboy. I never heard of that.

MICHAEL: Well, he's not your science fiction alien. He's a real alien and he has a real life. Not an interesting one necessarily, but a life.

SHERIFF: Where is he now?

MICHAEL: *(Beat)* I don't know.

SHERIFF: No idea?

MICHAEL: No.

SHERIFF: He just left, just like that? Not a word?

MICHAEL: That's right.

SHERIFF: Any guesses which way he was heading?

MICHAEL: Look, they're an advanced race, okay? I don't pretend to know what one of them might be thinking. They're very subtle, very brilliant.

SHERIFF: I thought he was a busboy.

MICHAEL: Well, I'm talking about potential.

SHERIFF: And I'm talking about where he went. Does he drive a car?

MICHAEL: I doubt it.

SHERIFF: So he's hitchhiking.

MICHAEL: Maybe, but I don't think anybody's going to pick him up.

SHERIFF: Why not?

MICHAEL: He has green skin.

SHERIFF: *(Gets an odd look on his face)* Trinkle.

MICHAEL: Excuse me?

SHERIFF: Mrs Trinkle. High school.

MICHAEL: Yeah...?

SHERIFF: You said green skin, and Mrs Trinkle just popped into my head. How do you like that? We did yearbook with her.

MICHAEL: Right. And Senior English.

SHERIFF: Good times. Good years. Huh. Now why the heck do you suppose that came back to me right then?

MICHAEL: Little Proustian moment I guess.

SHERIFF: Yeah, I guess so...a what?

MICHAEL: Never mind, nothing.

SHERIFF: Seems like a long time, doesn't it.

MICHAEL: It is a long time.

SHERIFF: Be nice to go back, though, wouldn't it.

MICHAEL: No, not really.

SHERIFF: We always thought a lot of you, Michael. Always thought you were the one going somewhere. That you were going to get out into the big world.

MICHAEL: Well, I didn't.

SHERIFF: No. You're still here, working at the K-Mart.

MICHAEL: You don't lose your provincialism by leaving the provinces, Hank. This is my big world, right here. *(Referring to the book)* At least, it's the place I go looking for the big world. I'm not sure I've found it yet.

SHERIFF: Don't you think you'd be better off leaving, though? Going off to Chicago, Minneapolis, New York? Someplace where people could...appreciate you?

MICHAEL: What makes you think they would? Wherever you go, they're still people, aren't they.

SHERIFF: You're frustrated Michael, and you're angry. You want people to understand you, but they don't, and they never will. Not around here.

MICHAEL: So what's this? Is the sheriff telling me to "get out of town"?

SHERIFF: Actually, the sheriff is saying stay put until this whole thing is over. Then get out of town. Find another town—a town where you can be happy, where you fit in. For yourself, I'm talking.

MICHAEL: Sure, no problem. Just one thing.

SHERIFF: What's that?

MICHAEL: Show me the town.

(Lights fade on them.)

Scene Four

(A roadside bar. Lots of different beer signs and a jukebox that doesn't work quite right.)

(RAY is behind the bar. THE ALIEN sits on a barstool, a glass of tap beer in one hand. Something about the lighting of the bar makes his skin look like it's a normal color.)

(10:30 A M)

(THE ALIEN is peering intently at the jukebox. He takes a swig of the tap. When he speaks, it's increasingly rapid fire, as if he's wired on caffeine.)

ALIEN: Hey, what is that thing? That is really cool looking.

RAY: What—you never seen a jukebox before?

(THE ALIEN turns back to it in wonder.)

ALIEN: Oh, a jukebox, a jukebox. Oh man! A jukebox! I heard of those, it's a jukebox. This is incredible.

RAY: 'Course, that one there has the karaoke feature.

ALIEN: No, you're kidding, oh my God, karaoke.
(He polishes off the tap and goes for a closer look.)

RAY: Oh yeah, we keep up with all the big city trends.

ALIEN: I didn't know if there really was such a thing
as karaoke, I mean you hear about karaoke but you're
not really sure if something like it really exists because
people make things up, you know? They make up all
kinds of great things and then you get to a place and it
isn't really there and then you're really disappointed
and then you get depressed and then you want to sing
karaoke even more than you did before, know what I
mean?

(RAY is already reaching to open another beer for THE
ALIEN.*)*

RAY: How's about one more?

ALIEN: I don't know—I'm pretty wired.

RAY: What the hey, gonna be noon before you know it.
And you look like you need a little somethin' to take
the edge off. *(Confidentially, as he hands* THE ALIEN *the
beer.)* I'd have one with you but it's against policy.

ALIEN: I thought you owned the place.

RAY: Well, yeah, I do. But the wife is management.
Final word is mine but management pretty much runs
the show. She says when I drink behind the bar, the
books don't balance at the end of the day.

ALIEN: And neither do you, I bet.

RAY: Eh?

ALIEN: Balance at the end of the day.

RAY: Oh dang. That's a good one. I got to tell the wife
that. You're quick on the come backs, ain't you. You

and she'd get along great. She's quick on the come
backs too.

(THE ALIEN *takes a deep swig as...the sound of a car pulling
into the lot outside.* RAY *goes to the window.*)

RAY: That'd be Hank. He's the Sheriff.

ALIEN: Sheriff?

RAY: He come by to talk to the wife. She and her ex are
goin' through some trouble on account of he says their
boy was abducted by Martians.

ALIEN: Abducted by *Martians...*

RAY: Yeah. How 'bout something original for cryin'
outside. *(He looks through the window. He waves and
talks—doesn't yell—through the window even though*
THE SHERIFF *obviously can't hear him.)* Yup, goin' right
around to the back door. Hey Hank. How ya doin'?

(Meanwhile, THE ALIEN *is visibly putting this all together
in his head.)*

ALIEN: How's she taking it?

RAY: Priscilla? Not so good. He done this before,
of course, but he never said it was Martians.
I'd say that was the part got her wound up.

ALIEN: Boy do I feel terrible.

RAY: How come?

ALIEN: Warmhearted by nature.

RAY: Oh.

ALIEN: I just wish there was something I could do.

RAY: When Priscilla's like this, she's in her own world.
There's no point in worryin' 'cause there's nothing
you're gonna do about it. My advice is you do what I
do—drop your dollar in there and sing your heart out.

ALIEN: No, I couldn't. I'm not much of a singer.

RAY: That's what they all say. You'll get the hang of it.

ALIEN: You first. You show me how.

RAY: Well I would but the problem is you don't get professional sound quality when the pipes are dry.

ALIEN: You're a professional singer?

RAY: Well, not exactly. But people're always asking me to get up and knock out an old ballad or two.

ALIEN: Is that right!

RAY: Well, I don't claim to be Mel Torme. But I can hold my own in these parts.

ALIEN: Oh, you have to sing for me! Please!

RAY: No, no. Wife wouldn't like it. Says the karaoke's for customers only.

ALIEN: I'll tell her I made you do it.

RAY: No, serious now. No can do 'less I get a couple in me—

ALIEN: Go on then—they're on me. (*He hands across a hundred dollar bill.*)

RAY: Dang.

ALIEN: And keep the change.

RAY: Well...maybe just one to get the vocal cords warmed up. How's she gonna know, eh?

ALIEN: Dang if I know!

RAY: Now you're talkin'. (*He pops open a beer and takes hit.*) First one of the morning sure tastes sweet, don't it?

ALIEN: Party...down!

(*Lights blackout.*)

Scene Five

(The office in back of the same bar. Time is continuous from the previous scene. THE SHERIFF *stands in the doorway, while* PRISCILLA *confronts him.)*

PRISCILLA: Do you know what Michael said to me two months ago? He had Billy for the afternoon and Billy threw a fit because Michael had thrown out his T V and he couldn't watch *The New Adventures of Hercules.* So Michael comes back to me and says if I keep letting him watch garbage like that, he's going to take matters into his own hands. His words: 'take matters into his own hands.'

SHERIFF: I think about throwing out my T V sometimes.

PRISCILLA: Excuse me, but you're missing the point.

SHERIFF: I think you're missing Michael's point.

PRISCILLA: I want to know what are you going to do about this.

SHERIFF: Well, I searched the woods, the clearing, the quarry. There's no sign of Billy out there.

PRISCILLA: Of course not. Michael wouldn't leave him in the woods. But I'll tell you what he might have done.

SHERIFF: What's that?

PRISCILLA: Drove Billy down to Sheboygan and left him with his Aunt Rho.

SHERIFF: Then why don't you go down there and get him?

PRISCILLA: Because I'm not playing this game with Michael again. He did this same thing last year. It took me three days to figure it out and I finally ended up on a two hour car trip to Sheboygan, listening to him lecture me about my parenting skills and my bad taste in T V shows. So this time, I'm putting it in the hands of the authorities.

That's you, by the way.

SHERIFF: I'm happy to go pay Aunt Rho a visit.

PRISCILLA: And if he's not there, I want you to arrest Michael.

SHERIFF: Priscilla, I think we could give that a day or two.

PRISCILLA: This is why I stuffed envelopes for your campaign? So you could tell me to wait a day or two?

SHERIFF: If we give him some time, he might just come around on his own.

PRISCILLA: I've got news for you, mister. Sheriffs get voted in and Sheriffs also get voted out. And I've got dirt on you, don't forget that. (*She collects her checkbook, purse, etc. and prepares to go out.*)

SHERIFF: There's no dirt on me.

PRISCILLA: You drive that county car when you go fishing up to Wabeno.

(THE SHERIFF *reacts.*)

PRISCILLA: Didn't think I knew that, did you. That's against regulations. I could use that in a campaign.

SHERIFF: What point are we trying to make here, exactly?

PRISCILLA: I have a son who is missing.

SHERIFF: You just said he's in Sheboygan with his Aunt Rho.

(*She is ready to go.*)

PRISCILLA: I said *maybe*. Now, by the time I get back from the wholesaler, I want movement on this. However you do it, that's up to you.

SHERIFF: Priscilla...

PRISCILLA: At least bring him into your office.

SHERIFF: And do what?

PRISCILLA: Put the pressure on, for cryin' out loud!

SHERIFF: I already did that. I stopped by this morning for coffee and I...

PRISCILLA: Hank, now listen. You set a mean speed trap, nobody can touch you on kittens in trees. But the Spanish Inquisition you are not. Can't you see that you've got to—

(RAY *enters.*)

RAY: Priscilla, we got any Blackberry Flavored Brandy in the storeroom?

PRISCILLA: You're interrupting, Ray.

RAY: Well, we got some out-of-towner wants to try Blackberry Flavored Brandy once.

PRISCILLA: You've been drinking, haven't you.

RAY: I ain't been drinking.

PRISCILLA: I smell it on your breath, you weasel.

RAY: I ain't been drinking.

PRISCILLA: If you start drinking up our profits again, I'll take your shotgun off the wall and kill you. Do you understand me?

RAY: (*To* THE SHERIFF) I hope you heard that, Hank. That's evidence.

PRISCILLA: Correction...I will divorce you, strip you of all your worldly possessions right down to your jockey

briefs, wait until January, and then throw your
fat-assed sorry-looking self into the snowbank. Then
I will take your shotgun and kill you. Are we clear?

RAY: And if I was fishin' right now, we wouldn't be
havin' this conversation! Now best you remember
who's the boss around here!

(PRISCILLA *makes a move at* RAY, *who flinches. To* THE
SHERIFF...)

RAY: I hope you saw that! *(He makes a fast exit.)*

SHERIFF: It's good to see you two are lettin' your
feelings out there.

PRISCILLA: Don't worry your pretty little head about my
feelings.

SHERIFF: Well sometimes I do.

PRISCILLA: You had your chance, big boy. It's a little late
for regret.

SHERIFF: Priscilla, I'm not talking about that.

PRISCILLA: You'd better not be!

SHERIFF: That was a very long time ago, Priscilla.
It was Junior Prom.

PRISCILLA: It was Homecoming.

SHERIFF: Well, I was sorry about it then and I'm sorry
now.

PRISCILLA: Me too. If you hadn't dumped me, I could be
married to you right now. Instead I married Michael on
the rebound. And then I married Ray on the rebound
from that. If this keeps up, I'm gonna marry my dog.

SHERIFF: I never dumped you.

PRISCILLA: You most certainly did.

SHERIFF: You're the one who broke it off.

PRISCILLA: Because I would not be humiliated by watching you ask Amy VanderHooven to Homecoming.

SHERIFF: You weren't even speaking to me.

PRISCILLA: Not after you asked Amy VanderHooven!

SHERIFF: Priscilla, this is ancient history. My own son Ethan is set to play in the Homecoming game this year and Amy VanderHooven went lesbian ten years ago. Now come on. We're here, you and me, right now.

PRISCILLA: You're right. Good. Current events then. Right now, Hank, you're the Sheriff. So arrest somebody. *(She exits before he can say anything.)*

(The lights change.)

Scene Six

(The bar. Some time has passed. THE ALIEN still sits on his bar stool. RAY is considerably drunker than before. RAY and THE ALIEN sing karaoke.)

RAY: *Volare, oh, oh!*

ALIEN: *Cantare, oh, oh, oh, oh!*
Nel blu, dipinto di blu
Felice di stare lassù grave...

RAY: We can sing in the glow of a star that I know of Where lovers enjoy peace of mind

RAY & ALIEN: *Volare, oh, oh!*
Cantare, oh, oh, oh, oh!

(The song ends.)

ALIEN: *Bravo! Eccellente!*

RAY: *(Modestly)* You're not so bad yourself there once.

ALIEN: *Dovresti cantare per tutta la vita!*

RAY: Not to mention you speak darn good Spanish.

ALIEN: *Grazie.*

RAY: Come to think of it, y'kinda have that olive compleshion. Ya got some Messcan in ya?

ALIEN: God I love this planet—place! I knew I was going to like it, but I had no idea! It's so...well, *earthy.* So...*honest.*

RAY: That's me.

ALIEN: Do you mind if I ask you something?

RAY: Yeah, sure. I got to siddown though... *(He discovers he's already sitting.)* Okay, shoot.

ALIEN: Suppose some friends of yours did something...upsetting.

RAY: All my frien's are out fishin'.

ALIEN: How about your wife?

RAY: She hates fishin'.

ALIEN: Well, how about the Sheriff?

RAY: Hank likes fishin'.

ALIEN: Okay. Suppose Hank—I don't know—kidnapped somebody.

RAY: He can't do tha', he's th' Sheriff.

ALIEN: It's hypothetical.

RAY: Oh! Awright. I'm with ya.

ALIEN: And you helped him.

RAY: Yeah, tha's *good.*

ALIEN: Not directly, but you provided certain services. But things got a little complicated and people got really wound up about it. In other words you feel just a little bit guilty.

RAY: Guilty!? Hah! I know all about guilty.

ALIEN: Expand.

RAY: Guilty is you promise your best darn fishin' buddies in the whole world that you're gonna spend a couple days at the Flowage, and then you gotta chuck the whole deal at the last second because you're too darn *accommodatin'* to the ball and chain! You're lookin' at somebody with some *issues* here, so don't tell me.

ALIEN: So there's nothing to be done.

RAY: I never said that.

ALIEN: Well what the hey. I'm relyin' on you for the local custom.

RAY: *(With great seriousness)* Canned goods.

ALIEN: Excuse me?

RAY: Nice package of canned goods usually puts it right. *(He places a six pack of bottled beer on the bar.)* Bottles're good too.

ALIEN: What if the situation is touchier than that.

RAY: I'd just go in there, put my arms around 'em, and jes' give 'em a big hug.

ALIEN: What you're saying is, provide comfort.

RAY: Yah.

ALIEN: You know what? You've got a beautiful soul.

RAY: *(Singing)* When the moon hits your eye...

ALIEN: *(Singing)* Like a big pizza pie...

RAY & ALIEN: That's amore!

(Lights change)

Scene Seven

(K-Mart, MICHAEL's *place of work.* MICHAEL *is stacking toy flying saucers onto the shelf.* THE SHERIFF *hands him boxes.)*

MICHAEL: So Billy shows up for the weekend, and flips out because I threw out the T V and he can't watch that Hercules crap—which apparently Ray told him was just like reading classical literature.

Inside, part of me dies. The other part is going to dismember Ray.

SHERIFF: All the kids watch that stuff, Michael.

MICHAEL: This is my son—my flesh and blood, a boy who walked to the C D player when he was five years old and put on Beethoven's *Seventh Symphony* all by himself.

SHERIFF: Well at least it wasn't *Xena: Warrior Princess.* That one's got too much sex and violence.

MICHAEL: Hank, you're missing the point.

SHERIFF: Well I think you're missing Priscilla's point.

MICHAEL: That *Hercules* show takes a timeless myth that penetrates to the core of our collective psyche, rips out every shred of meaning, and gives us back the empty shell. The myth of Hercules is about guilt and courage and innocence and rage—and sex and violence for that matter, but real sex and real violence. With real causes and real consequences. That T V show is about a guy with big muscles and long hair!

SHERIFF: Well sex and violence wasn't the same thing in the old days.

MICHAEL: What are you talking about?

SHERIFF: They weren't so down and dirty back then.

MICHAEL: Are you kidding?! What about *Anna Karenina*?

SHERIFF: If that's on cable, we don't get that...

MICHAEL: *Anna Karenina*. It's a book. It was an assignment senior year!

SHERIFF: Well I never got to it!

MICHAEL: *Hamlet* then! We had that too! *A Streetcar Named Desire*! *Crime and Punishment*!

SHERIFF: Okay I get the...

MICHAEL: *The Iliad*! *The Odyssey*! *The Bible*!

SHERIFF: Michael, okay.

MICHAEL: Sex and violence galore!

SHERIFF: Okay, I got it.

MICHAEL: You don't got it.

SHERIFF: I'm not a total rock head, Michael. I got it!

MICHAEL: Priscilla was never like this when she was with me! It's Ray's fault.

SHERIFF: Priscilla is happy in her new life, Michael. One of these days you have to accept that.

MICHAEL: She is not happy with him.

SHERIFF: Priscilla's as happy as Priscilla gets. She's not an easy woman to please.

MICHAEL: I pleased her.

SHERIFF: Well, apparently—no.

MICHAEL: I was good for her.

SHERIFF: She divorced you.

MICHAEL: Ultimately, yes, but in the meantime we had some good years.

SHERIFF: No you didn't.

MICHAEL: Well—months, anyway.

SHERIFF: Everything always comes back to Priscilla in your mind. You're fixated on her. You've got to let go of that anger.

  Now look, I want to clear up a couple things before I head to Sheboygan. Did you threaten to take Billy if he, uh... *(He consults a notebook.)* ...if his home environment didn't get better?

MICHAEL: Did she tell you that?

SHERIFF: Yes or no?

MICHAEL: I was just spouting off about Ray. She knows that.

SHERIFF: What's so bad about Ray? He's a solid guy.

MICHAEL: He's a moron.

SHERIFF: He's a typical, regular guy.

MICHAEL: Exactly.

SHERIFF: All right, now look. I got to ask you to come down to the station for a few minutes.

MICHAEL: The station?

SHERIFF: I am conducting an investigation. It's standard procedure.

MICHAEL: You've been waiting for this for twenty years, haven't you! Ever since I quit the bowling team to take oboe lessons.

SHERIFF: Will you please come down with me?

MICHAEL: No.

SHERIFF: Michael, I'm asking you nicely.

MICHAEL: Well, are you asking me or telling me?

SHERIFF: I'm asking you.

MICHAEL: I'm not going down to the station with any guy who's never read *Anna Karenina*.

SHERIFF: Michael, I don't want to arrest you.

MICHAEL: Why not?

SHERIFF: I don't want to do the paper work.

MICHAEL: Then I'm not going.

SHERIFF: *(Beat)* All right, all right. I'll meet you half way. How's that?

MICHAEL: How's what?

SHERIFF: You come down to the station by your own choice—no fuss, and I'll read that, uh, Anna Kara-what's-her-name for you.

MICHAEL: You're kidding me, right?

SHERIFF: I'm dead serious. No guarantee I'm going to understand it, mind you. But I'll crack the old binding there. Or if you insist, we'll do it the old fashioned way. It's up to you.

MICHAEL: Hank, this whole thing is unfair. It's embarrassing and it's downright unfriendly. But the thought of you reading *Anna Karenina* almost makes it worthwhile.

SHERIFF: So is it a deal?

(MICHAEL *gestures for him to lead the way.*)

MICHAEL: Take me to your leader.

(MICHAEL *exits, followed by* THE SHERIFF.)

(*The lights cross fade.*)

Scene Eight

(The bar. RAY is asleep—passed out—on the top of the bar. He snores. THE ALIEN finishes off his beer and walks around to the back of the bar. He pours himself a big cup of coffee.)

(He's about to drink it when PRISCILLA appears behind him, coming in from the back with a carton of bottles.)

PRISCILLA: And just what do you think you're doing?

ALIEN: Oh. I paid for this.

PRISCILLA: What am I, stupid? Get out from behind there.

ALIEN: You can ask, Ray. I paid in advance. I'm covered.

PRISCILLA: Mister, don't mess with me. The Sheriff's a friend of mine and I've got a twelve gauge right back there. Now move it on out.

ALIEN: Under protest.

PRISCILLA: Under anything you want, just do it.

(He comes out from behind the bar. She goes behind it herself.)

ALIEN: You must be Priscilla.

(RAY snorts.)

ALIEN: Ray here speaks highly of you.

PRISCILLA: Ray here drinks in the middle of the day.

ALIEN: So do I.

PRISCILLA: Some people can hold it.

ALIEN: It did seem to knock him up.

PRISCILLA: Out.

ALIEN: What?

PRISCILLA: Knock him out.

ALIEN: Right. Knock him *out.*

PRISCILLA: Any excuse to take a nap or go limp.
That's my Ray.

(RAY *snorts.*)

ALIEN: I need to say two things. First, this is my fault
and I'm sorry. Don't be angry with him. If you must
be angry with someone, I'm the one.

PRISCILLA: What's the other thing?

ALIEN: You're unhappy.

PRISCILLA: Yeah, well—you would be too, believe me.

ALIEN: Yes, Ray told me about Billy. But that's not what
I meant. I meant something deeper. Something very
basic.

PRISCILLA: My emotional condition is none of your
concern.

ALIEN: But it is my concern. No man is an island, entire
of itself; every man is a piece of the continent, a part of
the main; if a clod be washed away by the sea, Europe
is the less, as well as if a promontory were, as well as
if a manor of thy friend's or of thy own were; any
man's death diminishes me, because I am involved in
mankind; and therefore never send to know for whom
the bell tolls; it tolls for thee.

PRISCILLA: *(Fascinated, softening in spite of herself)*
Not local, are you.

ALIEN: No, but I like the neighborhood.

PRISCILLA: You ought to be meet my ex-husband.
You and he'd get along great.

ALIEN: I'm not so sure about that. I bet he prefers
women.

(She laughs out loud.)

PRISCILLA: Last time I checked.

(Pause. They look at each other. She's unsure of herself but liking it.)

ALIEN: I thought you were leaving.

ALIEN: We were discussing your melancholy state of mind.

PRISCILLA: Nice of you to care—but what makes you so interested?

ALIEN: I told you. I am involved in mankind.

PRISCILLA: Oh yeah. I'm impressed by the way. You know that whole speech. How did that happen?

ALIEN: No, let's talk about you instead.

PRISCILLA: Uh-unh.

ALIEN: I memorized it.

PRISCILLA: Why?

ALIEN: Your turn. Tell me your sorrows.

PRISCILLA: No. Why did you memorize it?

ALIEN: Because I had to. They made me.

PRISCILLA: They?

ALIEN: My...employers. It was part of a training program. They made us learn all kinds of information about your, our world. You know—culture, science, mating rituals. I couldn't care less about it, to tell you the truth. Except for that one part. "I am involved." That part I get.

(Beat)

PRISCILLA: Life stinks.

ALIEN: Expand.

PRISCILLA: You divorce your husband number one and he kidnaps your little boy. And the Sheriff who dumped you just before Homecoming, and who you helped get elected to office, won't lift a finger to get him back. Then there's hubbie number two, who you married because he impressed you by being outdoorsy and fun-loving and he looked great on a Harley—only now you can't even leave him in charge of the family business for two hours but you come back to find him in his usual state of arousal.

(She indicates RAY, *passed out. He snorts.)*

ALIEN: But a hundred dollars richer.

(She looks and finds the money.)

ALIEN: Told you—I paid in advance.

PRISCILLA: What do you do? Print it yourself?

ALIEN: No, other people do that for me.

PRISCILLA: Oh, rich kid, huh?

ALIEN: Rich enough to take you away from all this.

PRISCILLA: Yeah? Where would we go?

ALIEN: How about to the moon and back?

PRISCILLA: I want to go wherever my kid is.

ALIEN: Oh.

PRISCILLA: Can't manage that one, can you.

ALIEN: No. Not really.

PRISCILLA: Didn't think so.

ALIEN: But I'm sure he'll be back.

PRISCILLA: You're very nice but your being sure is just not good enough.

ALIEN: I promise you, he'll come back. All safe and sound.

PRISCILLA: Listen, what do you know? Huh? You don't have a crazy ex-husband and you probably don't have kids either, do you. So what would you know? Huh? What would you know about these feelings? You don't know anything.

ALIEN: I'm sorry you're upset.

PRISCILLA: One thing I don't need is sympathy!

ALIEN: Yes it is.

PRISCILLA: No it is not!

ALIEN: Everybody needs sympathy.

PRISCILLA: I am not everybody. I am Priscilla Zuelke. *(Pronounced ZULL-key. Rhymes with FULL-key)* I do not need anything, anytime, from anyone.

ALIEN: Then what do you want?

PRISCILLA: Someone who'll listen to me when I talk.

ALIEN: It must be awful, not having anyone to listen.

PRISCILLA: It is awful!

ALIEN: Of course it is.

PRISCILLA: You don't know. It's always me who has to listen and I can't do it anymore! It's...it's...it's...!

(She breaks down and cries.)

ALIEN: Go ahead. Have a good cry.

(She cries. He strokes her shoulder.)

ALIEN: That's right. Let it out. Let it out.

PRISCILLA: Oh God! It's...too much!

ALIEN: Yes, it is.

PRISCILLA: It's too much for one person!

ALIEN: It is, you're right. It isn't fair. *(He moves in closer and embraces her lightly.)* You've been very brave.

PRISCILLA: No I haven't.

ALIEN: Yes, you've kept a very level head through all of this.

PRISCILLA: How would you know?

ALIEN: I've got eyes. I see how you are. You're strong. But when it's too much, it's too much. A person can only take so much.

PRISCILLA: That's right. *(She stops crying.)* You're touching me.

ALIEN: Is it all right?

PRISCILLA: Well, no, not really.

ALIEN: Why not?

PRISCILLA: Because my husband is right there.

ALIEN: He's asleep.

PRISCILLA: People wake up.

ALIEN: Eventually.

PRISCILLA: No really. I...I didn't want this.

ALIEN: I know. But I can't help it. I listened.

PRISCILLA: But Ray...

ALIEN: I can't help you there. But I can help you here.

PRISCILLA: Oh...

ALIEN: If you want me to.

PRISCILLA: I...I don't know...

ALIEN: I think you do know.

PRISCILLA: I think I do too. *(She kisses him, then pulls away.)* Not here.

ALIEN: Yes.

PRISCILLA: No, there's an apartment upstairs.

ALIEN: I don't like apartments.

PRISCILLA: But...

ALIEN: He won't wake up for hours.

PRISCILLA: How do you know?

ALIEN: I know. I know more than you think.

(He presses her against the bar, kisses her passionately, and they begin to make love.)

(Lights fade.)

Scene Nine

(The same, evening. MICHAEL is at the front door. He sees RAY asleep on the bar.)

MICHAEL: Hey. Wake up. Wake up. Ray, wake up.

RAY: Oh gawd...

MICHAEL: Come on. Wake up.

RAY: Pr'cilla's not here.

MICHAEL: I'm not looking for Priscilla.

RAY: Well, sh'snot here.

MICHAEL: Will you please wake up?

RAY: I'm'wake.

(But his eyes stay shut. MICHAEL walks around the bar, pours a glass of water and throws it in RAY's face. RAY opens his eyes.)

RAY: Thank you.

MICHAEL: I thought you stopped drinking during the day.

RAY: This was social. I was pressured.

MICHAEL: By whom?

RAY: Some drunk, that's whom. Who else stands outside a bar at 10 o'clock in the morning?

MICHAEL: How did he look?

RAY: He looked like a drunk with a bad case of liver damage. Worst looking skin I ever saw.

MICHAEL: Sort of...green?

RAY: I'd say more like yellow. Inside the bar here, he didn't look so bad—neon lights, you know. But outside in the daylight...whoo-ee. Scary. Hell of a nice guy, though. (*He goes behind the bar and pours himself a little hair of the dog.*)

MICHAEL: Where did he go?

RAY: I don't know.

MICHAEL: When did he leave?

RAY: I don't know.

MICHAEL: You mean, you passed out while he was still here?

RAY: When you pass out, you don't have much say over when.

MICHAEL: Did he say where he was going?

RAY: He just said he had to take off.

MICHAEL: Take off?

RAY: Yeah, get goin'.

MICHAEL: Well, did he say "get going," or did he say "take off"?

RAY: What difference does it make? He left, okay?

MICHAEL: It makes a lot of difference!

RAY: Well I can't remember.

MICHAEL: Well, the first time you said "take off".

RAY: Okay.

MICHAEL: So is that it? Is that what he said?

RAY: Yeah. Okay? That's what he said.

MICHAEL: You don't even know, do you?

RAY: No, I don't know! The rest of us aren't so perfect, Mike. I never went to college, I don't take notes!

MICHAEL: That's not what this is about!

RAY: Oh really? Then what's it about?

MICHAEL: That drunk was an alien! He's one of them, you dolt! He was at my house this morning. I got angry and like an idiot I let him walk out on me, and now I have absolutely no idea where he is and he's my only contact with Billy, so it's somewhat crucial that I find him!

(Slight pause)

RAY: Holy moley—you're really all holes and no cheese, ain't ya?

MICHAEL: Didn't it occur to you even once? You sat there and listened to me last night talking about the aliens and how they took Billy, and this morning a green-skinned man shows up at your bar?

RAY: I didn't say green, I said yellow. Liver damage don't make you green.

MICHAEL: But maybe this wasn't liver damage, Ray.

RAY: Hey, gimme some credit one time. I know something on the subject, okay? This guy was yellow.

MICHAEL: That's because you see the world through the light of an Old Milwaukee sign!

RAY: I took your wife, Mike. Okay? I'm sorry about that. But there's no need to get personal.

MICHAEL: You did not take Priscilla.

RAY: Well, she's married to me, whether anybody likes it or not.

MICHAEL: Priscilla left me, Ray. You had nothing to do with it! *(He starts to leave.)*

RAY: You never loved her.

(MICHAEL stops.)

MICHAEL: I loved her.

RAY: Well you sure as heck never understood her.

MICHAEL: I understood her. Better than you ever will. There's a song inside her and someday she's going to sing it and believe me, the tune will not be Ray Zuelke.

(MICHAEL exits. RAY calls after him.)

RAY: Well boo-hoo! You're really breakin' my heart! And what's more, Priscilla's tone-deaf!

(We hear PRISCILLA's lovely voice from the back, singing. RAY meanwhile gets a cold cloth from behind the bar. He sits down in a chair and presses the cloth across his eyes as PRISCILLA enters.)

PRISCILLA: "Blue moon
You saw me standing alone
Without a dream in my heart
Without a—

(She sees RAY, who has taken off the cloth and is looking at her.)

PRISCILLA: Oh. Hello.

RAY: I'm sorry, Priscilla.

PRISCILLA: Sit, sit. *(She puts a fresh cloth on him.)*
I'll get you fresh.

RAY: Priscilla, if you're winding up for the pitch,
go ahead and let fly. I'm ready for it.

PRISCILLA: What pitch? Head back.

RAY: About how I uh—took a little nap at the bar.

PRISCILLA: "Got drunk and passed out" you mean,
don't you.

RAY: Yes Priscilla.

PRISCILLA: I know we have our troubles, Ray. And I
don't know where it goes from here, but from now on,
let's both of us say what we mean and mean what we
say.

RAY: Yeah, okay. I know you're angry at me.

PRISCILLA: Ray, I'm not angry.

RAY: You're not?

PRISCILLA: Sometimes the world is a surprising place.
Unplanned. Beautiful. And if you let yourself be
surprised, if you're unafraid, if you accept that
anything is possible but that nothing is certain, then
you can really live. We spend most of our lives turning
away from that ecstacy, denying it, refusing it. Fearing
it. It's too beautiful, it asks too much of us. But when
we find it—
   Angry Ray? I just can't find it in myself.

RAY: Priscilla.

PRISCILLA: Yes, Ray.

RAY: *(Testing)* I'm goin' to meet the boys tomorrow
morning up to the Flowage.

PRISCILLA: That sounds lovely.

RAY: The Flowage, Priscilla, real early—and we won't get back 'til late.

PRISCILLA: Have a wonderful time. *Arrivederci!*
(She kisses him on the forehead.)

(Lights fade)

Scene Ten

(A clearing in the woods. THE ALIEN *sits, reading an Us magazine, and wearing a Walkman.* MICHAEL *enters in a hurry. He stops abruptly when he sees* THE ALIEN.)

MICHAEL: I knew it! I've been looking all over for you! You're waiting for them, aren't you. They're coming back.

ALIEN: No comment.

MICHAEL: Why else would you be out here?

ALIEN: Michael, it would be better if you went home.

MICHAEL: I'm staying right where I am. I want to be here when Billy steps off that ship.

*(*THE ALIEN *offers no further resistance.* MICHAEL *sighs, annoyed, and sits down.)*

MICHAEL: I should have brought a jacket. Don't you get cold?

ALIEN: All the time.

MICHAEL: You don't look cold.

ALIEN: You get used to it.

MICHAEL: I guess it's always cold in outer space.

ALIEN: Yeah, and no one can hear you scream either. That movie scared the crap out of me. Checked under my bunk for a month.

MICHAEL: How do you know all these movies, anyway?

ALIEN: The T V signal. It doesn't stop when it gets to
your T V set, you know. It keeps going, out into space.

MICHAEL: No. *(Beat)* So I'm not supposed to be here
when they bring him back.

ALIEN: Not really, no.

MICHAEL: I was here when they took him, wasn't I?

ALIEN: That was a mistake.

MICHAEL: So they make mistakes.

ALIEN: Are you kidding? Why do you think we keep
coming back? Because interstellar travel is such a treat?
Because our thirst for knowledge cannot be assuaged?
No. Because they can't get it right. That's why.

MICHAEL: What have you got to be so bitter about?

ALIEN: All my life, I was subjected to all the snooty
high brow culture you can imagine: Ludwig Van
Beethoven—

MICHAEL: They know Beethoven?

ALIEN: They love Beethoven. And Shakespeare
and Ibsen. And Marxist theory, Plato and Aristotle,
Rembrandt and Titian, Goethe and Dickens and Tolstoy
and blah dee blah dee blah!
    But Michael, all I wanted was to listen to The Spice
Girls, to flip through the new *Us* Magazine, to watch
Friends. That's what I came down here for. Is that such
a terrible thing?

MICHAEL: I wouldn't say terrible—but is it worth
coming all the way across the galaxy for?

ALIEN: To me, it is. Anyway, I had one good day. I wish
there'd be a few more, that's all. *(He stands up suddenly.)*
Hold on! Hold on!...

MICHAEL: What's wrong?

ALIEN: I'm getting a message.

MICHAEL: What kind of message?

ALIEN: Shh! *(Beat)* They're not coming. They're turning back.

MICHAEL: What?

ALIEN: Further tests.

MICHAEL: They can't do that.

ALIEN: They just did.

MICHAEL: Oh come on!

ALIEN: I'm sorry! They just sent word.

MICHAEL: Just when sent word? You have a radio?

ALIEN: It's not a radio.

MICHAEL: Well, what is it?

ALIEN: It's this doohickey.

MICHAEL: A doohickey?

ALIEN: A Telepathy Enhancement Device. They send messages and I listen.

MICHAEL: If you're AWOL, how do they know to be sending you messages?

ALIEN: They're not sending me messages. It's an open channel. I get everything.

MICHAEL: Well, I don't see any doohickey.

ALIEN: It's implanted.

MICHAEL: Where?

ALIEN: *(With his finger in his mouth)* Ith in 'ere.

MICHAEL: Look, I want him back. I want my son back! *(He moves closer, grabbing* THE ALIEN.*)*

ALIEN: You'll get him back! Don't worry about it!

MICHAEL: When?!

ALIEN: Before sunrise!

MICHAEL: Which sunrise?

ALIEN: I don't know!

MICHAEL: Well, ask them!

ALIEN: How can I ask them?!

MICHAEL: Use the doohickey.

ALIEN: It doesn't work that way. You can't talk into it.

MICHAEL: What kind of radio is that, you can't talk into it. *(He threatens* THE ALIEN *physically again.)*

ALIEN: It's not a radio, and it's one-way! They talk to me, I can't talk to them!

MICHAEL: You're lying to me!

ALIEN: Why would I lie!?

MICHAEL: Because it doesn't make any sense! What if you were in trouble? What if you needed help? What if somebody were going to kill you? Huh?

ALIEN: You wouldn't hurt me. You're bluffing.

MICHAEL: Wouldn't I?

ALIEN: You wouldn't hurt a flea.

MICHAEL: But you're not a flea, you're an alien. What if I were just pissed off enough—what if I wanted my son back just enough that I said I was going to murder you if you didn't get him back here?! What would happen then? Would your little one way doohickey turn into a two way doohickey? Well?! *(Pause)* Well? Would it? *(He has* THE ALIEN *down on the ground now.)*

ALIEN: No!

MICHAEL: I'll kill you.

ALIEN: You wouldn't!

MICHAEL: I will if I have to! I'm not lying!

ALIEN: Yes you are!

MICHAEL: Do they hear you now? Do they hear
what you're saying? Do they hear what I'm saying?
(Into the void) Do you hear what I'm saying?!

ALIEN: No, they can't!

(MICHAEL *is still clutching him.*)

ALIEN: Don't you get it, Michael? It's because I don't
really matter. If they lose me, life goes on. The mission
goes on. I'm extra. I'm the throw away.
   That's who I am. You didn't get some cosmic Einstein,
some messiah from another planet. You got me.

(MICHAEL *lets go of him and stands. He looks up at the sky.*)

MICHAEL: I'm sorry.

ALIEN: Yeah. Me too.

MICHAEL: He's really not coming.

ALIEN: Not tonight.

(Pause)

MICHAEL: It's cold.

ALIEN: Yup.

MICHAEL: Well, I'm going back.

ALIEN: To sleep?

MICHAEL: If I can.

ALIEN: Sometimes you can't sleep?

MICHAEL: Not if I'm wound up.

ALIEN: Are you wound up?

MICHAEL: You could say that. Listen, why don't you come back to the house. We could talk.

ALIEN: What is there to talk about?

MICHAEL: You could tell me more about where you're from.

ALIEN: You don't want to know about that.

MICHAEL: How do you know?

ALIEN: It's boring. It's a boring place. They're all a bunch of boring self-important snobs. They're so self-important it makes me want to puke.

MICHAEL: Then come back and watch T V.

ALIEN: I thought you threw it out.

MICHAEL: I'll buy another one first thing in the morning. It'll be cheap, I've got employee discount.

ALIEN: You wouldn't mind?

MICHAEL: I could have had you tracked down, you know. You could be in the slammer right now. And I could have shown this whole town that I'm not loony tunes. But I didn't. I don't know why exactly—but there you go.
    Come back. I'll make some nice cold coffee. My special blend—French Roast with a hint of hazelnut.

ALIEN: What about you?

MICHAEL: I've got a very nice single malt I've been saving for the right occasion.

ALIEN: It's a deal.

MICHAEL: Come on, then. We'll listen to the radio. It's not much, but on a clear night I can pick up Chicago.

ALIEN: All the way to Chicago...! Impressive.

(MICHAEL *gestures for* THE ALIEN *to go ahead of him.* THE ALIEN *exits.* MICHAEL *is about to follow when he stops to look up at the sky.*)

(*The lights fade.*)

END OF ACT ONE

ACT TWO

Scene One

(A T V talk show set)

(MICHAEL sits on one chair, PRISCILLA in another. They're a few feet apart.)

(THE ALIEN stands off to one side, with a hand held mike. He has that slightly unctuous tone of a talk show host.)

ALIEN: We're back with Michael and Priscilla, and the question we're trying to deal with today is: what do you do when your ex-husband says he didn't kidnap your little boy—aliens did!

(Over MICHAEL's head a sign appears that reads "Says His Son Was Kidnapped By Aliens.")

ALIEN: But Priscilla his ex-wife, just isn't having any of it!

(Over PRISCILLA's head a sign that reads "Doesn't Believe A Word He Says.")

ALIEN: So, Priscilla—I have a question for you. Did he ever lie to you when you were married to him?

MICHAEL: I never lied to her.

PRISCILLA: This is my question.

MICHAEL: I never lied to her.

PRISCILLA: *(To THE ALIEN)* Would you tell him it's my turn?

ALIEN: Michael, please—you'll get your chance.

PRISCILLA: It wasn't that he lied, exactly.

MICHAEL: I never lied.

PRISCILLA: Let's just say he had certain problems perceiving reality.

MICHAEL: That is not true.

PRISCILLA: When we first got married, he told me that, when he was a little boy, he used to fly down off his roof.

MICHAEL: I never said that.

PRISCILLA: Yes you did Michael.

MICHAEL: I said it was like flying.

PRISCILLA: You always said, "I flew off the roof and went flying around the yard."

MICHAEL: Because that's how it felt. *(To* THE ALIEN*)* I built a home-made glider when I was a kid.

PRISCILLA: Sure, he tells you that. For years, I never heard the home-made glider part. All I ever heard was: "I flew off my roof."

MICHAEL: You used to love that story.

PRISCILLA: I used to love a lot of things about you until I found out you were a pathological liar. *(To* THE ALIEN*)* He used to make stuff up about our little boy too. Used to insist that Billy put on a Beethoven symphony when he was five years old, all by himself. Except Billy thought he was putting on the soundtrack to Beethoven, that St. Bernard movie!

ALIEN: Okay, okay. But we're looking for something really, deeply strange about Michael. Can you dig down, try to really give us something good?

PRISCILLA: *(Slight beat)* He once told me that he saw angels on the ceiling of the church.

MICHAEL: Because I did.

PRISCILLA: You did not.

MICHAEL: Yes I did.

PRISCILLA: No you didn't Michael.

MICHAEL: Yes I did. *(To* THE ALIEN*)* I saw them.

PRISCILLA: *(Throwing up her hands)* Uh!

*(*THE ALIEN *holds up the microphone to* THE SHERIFF, *who is in the audience.)*

ALIEN: Yes sir.

SHERIFF: *(Holding up* Anna Karenina.*)* Michael, this Anna Karenina is nothing but sex and violence.

ALIEN: *(Going back to* MICHAEL*)* Thank you.

SHERIFF: *(To* MICHAEL*)* And I'm lovin' every word of it! *(To "the camera")* Hello Ethan!

ALIEN: *(Back with* MICHAEL*)* So Michael, you saw actual angels on the ceiling of your church.

MICHAEL: I certainly did.

PRISCILLA: Nobody else saw them. All anybody else saw was the reflections of the sun off the windshields of cars that were passing by outside.

MICHAEL: I saw the same thing—it's just that I saw something more. I saw what those reflections meant!

PRISCILLA: You see? He admits he never saw angels!

MICHAEL: Priscilla, it's a metaphor. *(To* THE ALIEN*)* She pretends she doesn't know things, but she does.

PRISCILLA: And he's condescending!

MICHAEL: Condescending?! Because I give you credit?

(THE ALIEN *goes to* RAY, *also in the audience.*)

ALIEN: Yes sir, go ahead.

RAY: I got a question.

ALIEN: Go ahead.

RAY: My question is you don't know dick! Whaddya think of that?!

ALIEN: Thank you so much. *(Back to* MICHAEL*)* Michael, let me get this straight. You saw a metaphorical angel.

PRISCILLA: A normal person would say he made it up!

MICHAEL: That's right. Metaphorical.

ALIEN: But real angels are different than metaphorical ones, wouldn't you say?

MICHAEL: All angels are metaphorical. They are an expression of the deity.

PRISCILLA: You see how he gets? *(To* MICHAEL*)* You're a snob, you know that?

ALIEN: Priscilla, hold on a second...

PRISCILLA: *(To* THE ALIEN*)* That's exactly the way he talks to me all the time.

MICHAEL: Because you sell yourself short!

ALIEN: So you never saw a real angel. And you lied about that.

MICHAEL: I did not lie about it. I saw real angels.

ALIEN: But they were reflections of some kind of light.

MICHAEL: In my mind, they were real. And that's where angels are real—in your mind.

ALIEN: And the aliens, where are they? Where are they, Michael? In the spaceship—or in your mind? Hold that thought, Michael. We're going to take a break. Back after these messages! *(He exits.)*

MICHAEL: Aliens are nothing at all like angels. Aliens are just people who come from other planets. They're perfectly ordinary people.

PRISCILLA: *(To* MICHAEL*)* You got caught. He's smarter than you.

MICHAEL: A lot of people are smarter than I am.

PRISCILLA: You got your tit caught in the ringer, Michael. *(She stands up to leave.)*

MICHAEL: Where are you going? I'm on television! Don't leave me alone out here! Priscilla, you can't leave!

PRISCILLA: Got to run! I've got a little something in the oven.

(She stands up and we see she's pregnant. She exits.)

*(*MICHAEL *pursues her as far as the door. Throughout the next speech, the overhead signs lift out of sight, the lights change.)*

*(*MICHAEL *calls after her, frantically—)*

MICHAEL: I did fly! What I did was the same thing as flying. You have no grasp of metaphor! A metaphor is not unreal, it's just a different kind of reality. A deeper, truer kind, as a matter of fact, but you need a little imagination to get to it. And that's what's wrong with you and everybody else in this town. Lack of imagination. Fantasy is good, it's healthy, it's normal. And if you knew the first thing about medieval theology, you'd know I was right about angels, too. They are a manifestation of the deity, and so are our thoughts, so don't tell me I'm crazy just because I happen to believe in levels of reality that you can't begin to appreciate.

(He realizes he's no longer on the tv set, but back in his own house. It's night. At the same time, THE ALIEN *has entered looking decidedly queasy.)*

MICHAEL: What's wrong?

ALIEN: I'm sick....

MICHAEL: What's the matter?

ALIEN: Too many Gummy Bears and not enough fiber. How about you?

MICHAEL: Just...talking to myself—

ALIEN: I thought maybe you were doing your nightly dramatic reading of Ibsen.

MICHAEL: Taking a break, actually. *(He picks up a rather thick book.)* I'm on the last play.

ALIEN: When We Dead Awaken...

MICHAEL: You know it?

ALIEN: Very well, actually. I made them give it to me on C D-ROM because I hate to read, but Ibsen sort of grows on you.

MICHAEL: Are you sure you're not sick?

ALIEN: I went out for some fresh air and it suddenly hit me. What I'm missing up there on the ship, it's not pre-popped popcorn and a stack of Jackie Chan movies. Well, I am missing that actually, but there's something else. Something a little deeper. It took me ten days of total immersion in your civilization to make me realize—I love earth because I love the people. I want human contact.

MICHAEL: What's wrong, I don't qualify?

ALIEN: But you don't need me, Michael. You're just like them. You've got everything you want right here. Ibsen, Kierkegaard, Beethoven—
    Michael, I like you. *(Referring to all his pop culture junk...)* And I appreciate how you helped me out. But I'm not anything you want me to be.

MICHAEL: No one is what I want them to be. I'm not what I want me to be. But I could help you. You could learn to appreciate great literature. It's wonderful and exciting—it's—it's—

ALIEN: I know, it's "The eye of our dreams and the pilot of our souls."

MICHAEL: Yes! You do understand! And you just confessed to liking Ibsen....

ALIEN: Well, I—

MICHAEL: Come on try this with me just once. We could divide up the parts.

ALIEN: Michael, no—

MICHAEL: You're obviously a good reader. Why not just try it?

ALIEN: Michael because I just don't care!

(Beat)

MICHAEL: Right. Okay. I won't ever ask again.

ALIEN: Tomorrow morning, I'd like to go out.

MICHAEL: Where to?

ALIEN: Well, that first day—I made a friend.

MICHAEL: What kind of friend?

ALIEN: Just someone I liked.

MICHAEL: A female type friend?

ALIEN: Not that it matters, but yes.

MICHAEL: Nice.

ALIEN: You see, I don't know how much longer I have here, but I want to go find her, spend whatever time I have.

MICHAEL: Does she know you're an alien?

ALIEN: Not exactly. The lighting was dim.

MICHAEL: Well you can't go to her looking like that.

ALIEN: Like what?

MICHAEL: You skin is green.

ALIEN: She won't care about that. She's not that type.

MICHAEL: Look, let me go down to the drugstore in the morning and pick up some makeup. Just enough to give you rosy cheeks. I'll bring it home at lunch.

ALIEN: You don't mind?

MICHAEL: They already think I'm pretty strange downtown. Buying a little Maybelline won't make much difference now.

ALIEN: Thank you, Michael.

MICHAEL: Well...back to Henrik.

ALIEN: "We'll see what we've lost only when we dead awaken."

MICHAEL: You remember it?

ALIEN: It's Irene, isn't it? "We'll see that we've never really lived until now."

MICHAEL: And then high up in the mountains, we hear Maja singing—"I am free! I am free! I am free! No more living in cages for me!

MICHAEL & ALIEN: I am free as a bird! I am free!"

(Lights out.)

Scene Two

(K-Mart, later that morning. A Blue Light on the top of a pole. It's not on.)

(MICHAEL is up on a short stepladder. THE SHERIFF is beside the ladder carrying a yearbook and Anna Karenina.)

SHERIFF: I'm up to page forty on *Anna K.* by the way. It's not so bad but I'm only clockin' a chapter a day, 'cause I don't want Ethan to catch me with it and get interested. It's a little too racy for him.
   What are you doing?

MICHAEL: I'm going to electrocute myself.

I'm kidding. It's a broken blue light, Hank. K-Mart without an operational blue light is not K-Mart as we know it.

(THE SHERIFF holds the ladder.)

SHERIFF: I got to thinking about our little talk when I remembered Mrs Trinkle? What'd you call that moment?

MICHAEL: Proustian.

SHERIFF: Right. Something about that kept nagging at me. So I got out my old annuals. And I looked through them. And right there, in our junior year, we did a play. A Mrs Trinkle original—"M Is for Martian". You were in it. You remember what you played?

MICHAEL: ...yes.

SHERIFF: What did you play?

MICHAEL: Hank, this is not relevant.

SHERIFF: What did you play, Michael?

MICHAEL: The Martian.

SHERIFF: And what color skin did you have in the play?

MICHAEL: Green.

SHERIFF: That's right. Color picture right here in the annual.

MICHAEL: Well Sherlock, you've done it again. Time to break out the cocaine and play the violin.

SHERIFF: Michael, please, I am asking you one last time. What did you do with Billy!?

MICHAEL: I didn't do anything.

SHERIFF: Michael...

MICHAEL: Sometimes, Hank, things just happen. Things are imposed. Things we don't want. This is one of those things, Hank. I did not want Billy taken, she did not want Billy taken, you did not want Billy taken. But Billy was taken. It's none of our doing. And there's nothing we can do about it. This is not about psychology or human will. It's the quintessential existentialist crisis, Hank: what do you do when you can do nothing? You fix the Blue Light. So that even if the world frustrates you, even if you have no place to go, and no one to go to if you did—even then, at least there will still be a Blue Light Special. At least that.

SHERIFF: That's real good. Real nice.
    But I got some news of my own. This has been draggin' on for too long now and I've got a responsibility to the public to wrap things up. If Billy's not back by nine o'clock tonight, I'm going to have to lock you up.

MICHAEL: Of course you are.

SHERIFF: It'll be out of my hands then, Michael. That could mean no more visitation rights. You could even land in prison.

MICHAEL: Then why not arrest me right now? This isn't very good police work.

SHERIFF: It's lousy dang police work! It's called friendship! No matter what I do, I can't make you see that.

You've got this way of seeing the world that's so much more complicated and interesting and weird than anything I could ever dream up, but you can't see something as simple as that.

Now look, wherever you've got him, just bring Billy back. Then get out of here and go someplace where people might see the world the way you do.

Darn it, Michael, do yourself the favor. Or if that's not good enough, then do it for me. For friendship.

MICHAEL: *(Beat)* I'll think about it.

(THE SHERIFF *takes off his watch and hands it to him.*)

SHERIFF: You do that. Meantime, just so there's no confusion. Nine o'clock tonight, Michael. That's it.

(THE SHERIFF *leaves.* MICHAEL *reaches down and flips the switch on the Blue Light. It turns on as the lights fade.*)

Scene Three

(MICHAEL'*s house. Late afternoon*)

(MICHAEL *enters in his K-Mart uniform.* PRISCILLA *enters from inside the house.*)

MICHAEL: Hello. Trespassing, I see.

(*She folds her arms and studies him for a moment.*)

PRISCILLA: There's a man living here. People out on County G have seen him out in the yard, and upstairs at the window.

MICHAEL: Yes and?

PRISCILLA: Simple question: did you go gay? Is that it?

MICHAEL: I didn't go anywhere, Priscilla. That man is the alien.

PRISCILLA: I knew you were going to say that.

MICHAEL: I always said you were sharp, Priscilla.

PRISCILLA: You know, I've been very patient with you. I have not gotten hysterical—which I could have. I have not had you thrown in jail—which I could have. I have very patiently waited while Hank dragged his ass for ten days. Because deep down I knew you wouldn't let anything happen to our little boy. But if this...man has anything at all to do with Billy being gone—I don't care if he's from the moon or Milwaukee, there's going to be serious heck to pay.

(RAY *enters, talking.*)

RAY: I checked all through the attic, but I couldn't find anything else...well, well, well.

MICHAEL: What is going on here? Breaking and entering is a crime, you know.

RAY: We didn't break anything.

MICHAEL: That's not what it means, Ray.

PRISCILLA: All right now.

MICHAEL: He thought it meant that. Didn't you, Ray?

RAY: I'll show you what I meant...!

PRISCILLA: (*To* RAY) You go on outside. I'll deal with this.

MICHAEL: You're married to the missing link. You realize that.

RAY: If I wasn't so darned even-tempered, I'd have to have it out with you.

PRISCILLA: Ray, go home. I want to talk to Michael.

RAY: Oh no. He ain't gettin' away so easy this time.

MICHAEL: Get away with what?

RAY: *(To* PRISCILLA*)* Go on, show him.

PRISCILLA: It's fine, Ray, really. Just leave us alone.

RAY: Go on, show him what you found.

(PRISCILLA *produces a fistful of makeup in her hand.)*

RAY: Make-up—for girls. Now that's kinky, I don't care what you say.

MICHAEL: He wanted make-up to cover the green skin if he went out.

RAY: He's some kinda kinky guy you met, and now you're co-habitating.

MICHAEL: He's from another planet!

RAY: Which one?

PRISCILLA: Ray, please...

RAY: Which planet? Don't think about it now. Which one?

MICHAEL: I...

RAY: Mars? Jupiter?

MICHAEL: ...I don't know.

RAY: You don't know what planet he's from.

MICHAEL: No.

PRISCILLA: Ray...

RAY: You ever ask?

MICHAEL: No.

PRISCILLA: Ray, listen to me...

RAY: You never once thought to ask.

MICHAEL: No!

RAY: So you're shacked up with this guy, but you don't even know what planet he's from. Don't you want to know the kinda person you're having relations with? Huh? Mike?

PRISCILLA: Ray, go away. Now!

RAY: Fine. You want to side with the uh, what-do-you-call, 'promiscuous homosexual agenda' here, you go right ahead. But you better know one thing. Every item on the shelf has got a price. Every last one. And that goes for both o' youse. *(He exits.)*

PRISCILLA: I didn't come here to snoop. *(She follows RAY as far as the exit, watching to make sure he's gone.)*

MICHAEL: Well, you did a pretty good job of it.

PRISCILLA: Michael, I'm pregnant. *(Pause)* I missed my period last weekend, so I took the home test and I...I don't know what to do!

MICHAEL: Well, Priscilla, it can't be that bad. I mean, you've got Ray...

PRISCILLA: It's not Ray's.

MICHAEL: How do you know?

PRISCILLA: Believe me, I know.

MICHAEL: So you've been—stepping out...

PRISCILLA: No! Once. Ten days ago. Right after Billy... *(She looks at him, doesn't want to start a fight.)* ...was gone.

MICHAEL: Oh, really nice timing.

PRISCILLA: I was vulnerable! I was depressed and angry and very lonely. And this...person came along and made me feel like it was all okay. I don't know. It was like...magic. I can't explain. Michael, please, I'm coming to you because you're the only one I didn't think would judge.

MICHAEL: Who is he?

PRISCILLA: I don't know.

MICHAEL: You don't know his name?

PRISCILLA: He came into the bar one day, and one thing // led to another and I—

MICHAEL: *(Overlapping at //)* Came into the bar...?!

PRISCILLA: Yes.

MICHAEL: The day after Billy—?

PRISCILLA: I was confused, Michael. I felt so isolated. I was raw. He started quoting that Ernest Hemingway thing at me—for whom the bell tolls, that thing— and that's all I remember, basically.

MICHAEL: That's John Donne, Priscilla.

PRISCILLA: Whoever—I fell for it. He sort of reminded me of you, in a way.

MICHAEL: Me?!

PRISCILLA: You, but not you. Better than you. Different. Anyway we spent most the afternoon together. It was very strange, with Ray right there, passed out the whole time. But somehow, very right. The entire time I was with this man, I could feel myself changing, inside, deep inside—being rearranged, becoming the person I was always meant to be. I even stopped worrying about Billy. I didn't stop thinking about him, but I stopped worrying.

Then we said goodbye finally. He said he couldn't give me his number. I understood, of course. He never actually said he'd call, but of course I assumed—like the dupe that I am. *(She unconsciously touches her*

stomach.) I have to have it, Michael. You know me,
I couldn't not have it.

MICHAEL: What if I could find him for you?

PRISCILLA: What are you saying?

MICHAEL: I know who he is.

PRISCILLA: Well, who?

MICHAEL: No, I don't think I'd better tell you.

PRISCILLA: Why not?

MICHAEL: It's the...him.

PRISCILLA: Michael, we've had our problems. But I was
always under the impression that when push came to
shove we were still friends—that I could at least talk to
you.

Now listen to me: there are no aliens! Aliens did not
take Billy. You are not living with an alien. An alien
did not get me pregnant! This is the real world Michael,
and in the real world there are no such things as aliens!
Or angels! Or flying! Now if you have a shred of human
compassion in you, I'm begging you—stop running
away from reality, have a little gratitude for the fact
that I left you, and for once in your life help me!!

MICHAEL: Oh my god.

PRISCILLA: What?

MICHAEL: *(An epiphany)* I just realized—I don't love
you, Priscilla.

PRISCILLA: Well good.

MICHAEL: I don't love you.

PRISCILLA: I'm very glad.

MICHAEL: *(Clutching her back)* I mean, I really don't love
you.

PRISCILLA: Michael, I know that. Let go of me.

MICHAEL: I haven't loved you for years. I thought
I did—all this time. Because there you were...so
beautiful, so smart—don't roll your eyes—you are.
I couldn't believe that someone like you couldn't be
what I wanted. I kept thinking to myself—underneath
all these intense feelings of hostility, she must be the
woman for me. But now all of a sudden, it's so clear:
I don't love you! I only loved what I wanted you to be!
And I couldn't stand to see you go because I always
thought somehow, someday you'd be that person.
But you won't. I know that now! And I really don't
love you!

PRISCILLA: Well, I...I don't love you too.

MICHAEL: I know. Isn't it great?

*(He embraces her and she responds. They hold tight for a
moment.)*

PRISCILLA: Great. Now where is he?

*(THE ALIEN has entered through the front door during the
above, behind Priscilla's back. Michael points to him. She
turns to see him. He smiles at her, touching her on the arm.)*

ALIEN: Greetings earthling!

PRISCILLA: Eek! *(She grabs MICHAEL.)*

PRISCILLA: You're...you're—it's you.

ALIEN: Yes.

PRISCILLA: *(To MICHAEL)* You weren't making it up.

MICHAEL: No.

PRISCILLA: You were telling the truth. The whole time.

MICHAEL: Yes.

PRISCILLA: You don't have Billy.

MICHAEL: No.

PRISCILLA: He has Billy.

MICHAEL: No, the ones in the ship—they have Billy. This one's a busboy.

PRISCILLA: You're a busboy?

ALIEN: Yeah.

MICHAEL: He's an AWOL alien busboy.

PRISCILLA: *(Takes a step towards* THE ALIEN*)* You...asshole!

ALIEN: Is she talking to me?

MICHAEL: My guess is yeah.

PRISCILLA: *(Approaching him now)* Where's my son?

ALIEN: *(Backing away)* He's in the ship. He'll be back soon.

PRISCILLA: *(Pursuing)* Soon isn't good enough, mister. I've been very patient about this.

ALIEN: I know. You've been wonderful.

PRISCILLA: You get those friends of yours on the horn and you get my boy back.

ALIEN: I can't.

PRISCILLA: Sorry—don't understand "can't". Not familiar with that word.

ALIEN: It means not able!

PRISCILLA: *(Grabs him and puts him in a arm lock)* Oh really? And what if I took off your left arm and beat you over your head with the bloody stump? How would that affect your "not able"?

ALIEN: Michael, help me. She's hurting me!

MICHAEL: Priscilla, I already tried this. He can't.

(PRISCILLA *lets go of the* ALIEN.)

ALIEN: What did I do? *(To* MICHAEL*)* Did I hurt her in some way?

MICHAEL: Yes—you loved her, you left her, and you didn't call.

PRISCILLA: You might have told me you weren't human. That would be the considerate thing to do before sleeping with someone.

ALIEN: It never occurred to me. I didn't think it was important.

PRISCILLA: I'm having a baby, you jerk!

ALIEN: You are? I am?

(MICHAEL *nods yes.)*

ALIEN: I'm going to be a father?

PRISCILLA: Yes!

ALIEN: *(To* MICHAEL*)* I'm going to be a father.

MICHAEL: Yeah, I heard.

ALIEN: *(To* PRISCILLA, *warmly)* I'm going to be a father!

PRISCILLA: Don't give me the warm glow treatment, mister. You have reduced me to fodder for those magazines at the check-out line. Well I am not going to be just another notch in your ray gun, buddy!

ALIEN: Listen, you had something to do with it too.

PRISCILLA: You sweet-talked me.

ALIEN: You wanted to be sweet-talked.

PRISCILLA: You took advantage of my vulnerability.

ALIEN: I soothed your raw, anxious nerves. I made you feel better.

PRISCILLA: Sure—then you dumped me.

ALIEN: I was confused. It took me a few days.

PRISCILLA: Ten. But who's counting.

ALIEN: I had a lot to figure out. But I finally did.
Michael can tell you, I was just about to come to you.
I even had him buy make-up, so you wouldn't be too
startled.

PRISCILLA: So you were going to go on pretending to be
something you weren't.

ALIEN: You mean from earth?

PRISCILLA: Your skin looked normal in the bar.

ALIEN: Wait a second. This is that 'race' thing, isn't it.
That's very important to you. I read up on it.

MICHAEL: You read something?

ALIEN: Fine, it was a video.

PRISCILLA: This is not about 'race.'

ALIEN: Look, you have to understand—nobody else
in the entire galaxy has even heard of this concept.
We figure it's got to be some kind of weird
psychological quirk you people have to keep life
complicated and difficult. Almost as if you didn't
really want to be happy.

PRISCILLA: I'd love to be happy. I just want to know
what I'm sleeping with.

ALIEN: Well, wouldn't we all. It's a good thing I happen
to be the right gender for you. Otherwise you wouldn't
even give me a second look.

PRISCILLA: *(To* MICHAEL*)* He's kidding, right?

ALIEN: And the amazing thing is that you're able to
find somebody you actually like after you're done
eliminating all the people you've convinced yourself
aren't right for you.

But where I come from, we take a slightly simpler approach: you find somebody you like, and everything else—well, you work around it.
And I like you. Even if you are different. Because even in the ways that we're different, there are some pretty great ways that we seem to, sort of, uh...complement each other.

PRISCILLA: You make it sound so easy.

ALIEN: It is easy. This, anyway. Things that are really complicated, well—what can you do. But things that are simple, why not leave them simple?

(She looks at MICHAEL.)

MICHAEL: He's got a point.

PRISCILLA: You're an alien.

ALIEN: *(Sympathetically)* I know.

PRISCILLA: It's very hard to get past that.

ALIEN: *(Again)* I know.

PRISCILLA: You're green.

ALIEN: And you're pink.

PRISCILLA: Besides which, you're going to get back on your spaceship, and go flying off into the wild blue yonder.

ALIEN: Well, I've been thinking about that. I really don't like it with them. I mean, I love them. But I can't stand them.
And besides, now I've got a very good reason to stay.
(He goes to her.)

PRISCILLA: I'm a married woman.

ALIEN: Get a divorce.

PRISCILLA: Right. Okay.

But I'm not going to marry you. I'm on a very bad trend and I want to break it.

(They start to kiss.)

PRISCILLA: What kind of baby am I going to have?

ALIEN: The usual. Part you, part me.

PRISCILLA: Will he be tinted?

ALIEN: Don't worry—you and I are not the first— and they always get your skin color. I realize that's important.

PRISCILLA: You make me sound prejudiced.

ALIEN: Yes, but I like you anyway.

(They kiss. MICHAEL sighs happily.)

ALIEN: Hold on! Hold on!...

PRISCILLA: What's wrong?

ALIEN: Wait a second...

PRISCILLA: What is it?

ALIEN: Quiet please! I'm getting a.... They're on their way!

PRISCILLA: What?

ALIEN: The ship. It's coming back!

(Lights out.)

Scene Four

(The bar. RAY *is behind the bar, eyeing the barrel of the shotgun.* THE SHERIFF *is reading* Anna Karenina. *Out of the corner of his eye, he catches* RAY *aiming the gun at him.)*

SHERIFF: God darn it, Ray. Point that thing some other way, would you?

RAY: It ain't loaded.

SHERIFF: Yeah, but it's a good bet you are. Now put it the heck down. I'm trying to concentrate here.

(RAY lowers the gun, but hangs on to it.)

RAY: He could be halfway to Canada by now and you're busy readin' Tchaikovsky there.

*(*THE SHERIFF *indulgently closes the book, but keeps a finger at his place.)*

SHERIFF: What time is it?

RAY: 8:52.

SHERIFF: You didn't even look. It's not that late.

RAY: I guarantee, it's 8:52. I got a very accurate internal clock. Real fishermen all got very accurate internal clocks.

SHERIFF: They do?

RAY: Yup.

SHERIFF: Why is that?

RAY: So you be sure to make last call.

SHERIFF: Anyhow, it's not nine yet. *(He starts to open the book again.)*

RAY: You know, a lot of us do lousy jobs we don't like.

SHERIFF: *(Not looking up)* I realize that.

RAY: Don't mean we shirk our duty.

SHERIFF: I'm not shirking. I'm stalling. Check your watch. Go ahead.

(RAY checks his watch.)

RAY: It's 8:54.

SHERIFF: You're internal clock is slow.

RAY: No. The watch runs fast.

SHERIFF: Either way, it's still not time.

RAY: Well how much longer you gonna give him, for cryin' outside?

SHERIFF: Mind your own business.

(He opens the book again and starts to read. RAY provokes him ...)

RAY: What do you think—some alien spaceship's gonna bring Billy back?

SHERIFF: Possibly.

RAY: You don't believe in no spaceship.

SHERIFF: I believe in Michael. Anyway, a few hours won't make much difference one way or the other.

RAY: No, 'less he's heading for Canada.

SHERIFF: He's not heading for Canada.

RAY: You don't think so, huh?

SHERIFF: No, I don't think so. He's going to do the right thing and bring Billy back.

RAY: Yah?

SHERIFF: Yah.

RAY: You don't sound too sure.

SHERIFF: I'm pretty darn sure.

(Pause)

RAY: 8:56.

SHERIFF: *(Reading)* So?

RAY: So hows 'bout a drink?

SHERIFF: No thanks.

RAY: Come on, just you and me. Nobody's going to know.

SHERIFF: Can't drink on duty. Same as you, Ray.

RAY: Well, it ain't same as me tonight.

(RAY fixes a drink behind the bar. THE SHERIFF looks up, impressed.)

SHERIFF: I thought the uh...management didn't like that.

RAY: That was the old management. New management don't care what I do.

SHERIFF: What are you talkin'?

RAY: I fired the old management this afternoon.

SHERIFF: How'd she take it?

RAY: She don't know yet. But I figured it only made sense since her and me were gettin' a divorce.

SHERIFF: You're getting divorced?

RAY: Yup.

SHERIFF: How did she take that?

RAY: She don't know that yet either. Gonna tell her when she gets home tonight. She's gonna miss those long nights of pleasure, but she'll get over it. Say what you like about Priscilla, she knows the price of peanuts.

(He takes a long drink. THE SHERIFF opens his book.)

RAY: What is that thing, anyhow?

SHERIFF: See for yourself.

(THE SHERIFF hands him the book. RAY takes it and turns to the first page.)

RAY: "Happy families are all alike; every unhappy family is unhappy in its own way." *(He riffles through to the end of the book, then exchanges a significant look at THE SHERIFF.)*

SHERIFF: That's hittin' it square on the nose, ain't it hey.

RAY: Yah.

SHERIFF: What time is it?

RAY: 9:00.

SHERIFF: It's time.

(THE SHERIFF officiously heads for the door, followed by RAY who begins to take the shotgun with him.)

SHERIFF: And no duck hunting.

(RAY leaves the gun on the bar and they exit.)

(Lights fade.)

Scene Five

(The clearing in the woods)

(Twilight. THE ALIEN and PRISCILLA enter. MICHAEL lags behind a bit.)

ALIEN: We're here. This is it.

(They all stop. THE ALIEN checks the sky.)

PRISCILLA: Any sign?

ALIEN: Not yet. They're still pretty far out.

PRISCILLA: How you do know?

ALIEN: They send messages. I have this doohickey.

PRISCILLA: You mean like a radio?

ALIEN: Not really.

MICHAEL: Don't even try, okay?

PRISCILLA: But they're bringing Billy back, right?
For sure.

ALIEN: Of course. That's why they're coming.
And also—well, you know—

PRISCILLA: What?

ALIEN: They'll be looking for me. But I'm not going.
Not if I can help it.

PRISCILLA: Not if you...! You promised.

MICHAEL: It wouldn't be the first time he changed the
story.

ALIEN: *(To* PRISCILLA*)* But they really are coming this
time.

MICHAEL: Let's face it—you're the little alien who cried
ship.

ALIEN: I couldn't help it last time. They went back for
more tests.

PRISCILLA: Tests? What kind of tests?!

ALIEN: All different kinds. But the worst ones are those
tests where you have a ship going from Alpha Centauri
to Aldebaran at thirty light years an hour, and another
ship coming from Aldebaran to Alpha Centauri at sixty
light years an hour, and when do they pass each other?

PRISCILLA: They're giving him math tests?

ALIEN: I never said they were nice. *(To* MICHAEL*)* And
they can't change their minds this time because they're
low on gas. They'll only just get back home as it is.

MICHAEL: You see? You say things like that and we're supposed to believe you. Spaceships don't run on gas.

ALIEN: How would you know?

(The ship passes by overhead—noises and lights.)

ALIEN: Okay? Good enough? Now look—I don't want to go back. I want to stay.

PRISCILLA: Well, what are we going to do?

ALIEN: I don't know. The thing is that they can be very determined.

PRISCILLA: What does that mean?

ALIEN: If they want me back, they have their ways.

PRISCILLA: Well, we're going to have to hide you.

ALIEN: They'll look and they'll find me.

PRISCILLA: What if we took you back and put you in the basement? Or the silo at Michael's barn. Or an old fallout shelter! Would that work?

ALIEN: If I'm missing, they'll find me. Believe me.

PRISCILLA: *(To* MICHAEL*)* Well, think of something!

MICHAEL: What if they didn't think you were missing? What if we put somebody else on the ship, even if it wasn't you...I bet they'd just close the doors and take off.

ALIEN: That's it ? !

PRISCILLA: Michael...you can't...

MICHAEL: Yes, I can. *(To* THE ALIEN*)* Can't I.

ALIEN: Absolutely!

PRISCILLA: Michael, this is out of the question.

MICHAEL: No, don't you see? It's the answer to the question. I've finally got someplace to go.

PRISCILLA: But you don't know what you're doing! Not in a spaceship!

ALIEN: It's easy. Just one, crucial thing: serve from the left, take from the right.

MICHAEL: I'm not getting on that ship so I can be a busboy.

PRISCILLA: You're not getting on that ship, period.

ALIEN: Okay, here's what you do. Right after take off, go straight to the main control room and tell them what's up.

MICHAEL: Okay.

PRISCILLA: What if they don't like it? What if they get angry?

ALIEN: They don't really get angry. Condescending yes, but not angry. Anyway, they'll like Michael.

MICHAEL: You think so?

ALIEN: A lot more than they ever liked me. Just get them going on Beethoven or something.

PRISCILLA: They know Beethoven?

ALIEN & MICHAEL: They loooove Beethoven.

MICHAEL: Okay, so where's the control room?

ALIEN: Well, when you get inside, you take a right. Not your first right, that's the bathroom. The second right, it's a four way.

MICHAEL: The second right.

ALIEN: And you go down the corridor about...I don't know...I'm really bad at distances, but let's say a hundred feet.

MICHAEL: A hundred feet.

ALIEN: Maybe a hundred fifty.

MICHAEL: A hundred fifty.

ALIEN: Wait a second! There's a water fountain.
On your left is a water fountain.

MICHAEL: Water fountain on the left.

ALIEN: If you get to that, you went too far. So go back
about twenty feet and take a right.

MICHAEL: Okay, second right, then right again.

ALIEN: Well, no. I mean, if you went past it and got to
the water fountain and had to go back, then it's a right.
Right?

MICHAEL: Right.

ALIEN: But if you get it right the first time, then it's a left.

MICHAEL: Right.

ALIEN: Left. And you're there! Simple.

PRISCILLA: You're going to get lost.

ALIEN: You're going to make it.

PRISCILLA: You can't just go to another planet.
People don't do things like that.

MICHAEL: Maybe they should.

PRISCILLA: Michael, there are problems. I'll grant you
that. You have a hard time fitting in, but this is your
planet and you're staying right where you are!

MICHAEL: Everyday people are born in the wrong time
or the wrong place. It's very common, it's just that with
me it's a little more drastic. I can't go to another
century, Priscilla, but I can do this.

PRISCILLA: These are unusual circumstances. You're all
worked up. You haven't thought it through.

MICHAEL: I think about this every day of my life!
   Priscilla, don't you see? I suffer from culture shock in

the world of my birth. I'm like a refugee, a temporary resident, waiting for my visa application to go through so I can go home to where I belong. Now all of a sudden, somebody hands me a passport and all my papers, and says "now or never". I'll miss you but I have to go. I want to go.

  And not just for me, Priscilla. For you too. This is the one, best gift I'll ever give you. He's perfect for you. He's decent and honest and loves you for who you are, and he'll love Billy just the same way. And best of all he wants to be here.

  And let's face it, I love Billy, and he loves me. But only because he's the most patient boy on earth.

  Take the gift, Priscilla. It's the only thing I've ever given you that you really wanted.

(A bright light from offstage, sounds of a spaceship landing.)

ALIEN: They're coming down!

PRISCILLA: Michael, I'm worried. I can't help it.

MICHAEL: I'll send you a sign. How's that?

PRISCILLA: What kind of sign?

MICHAEL: I don't know. A signal. When you get it, it means everything's fine. Okay?
  Good bye.

(She grabs him and they embrace.)

MICHAEL: And uh—you too. *(He embraces* THE ALIEN *and turns to go.)*

ALIEN: Michael. Thank you.

(They lock gazes for a split second.)

(The ship lands.)

*(*THE ALIEN *ducks behind a log and Michael turns back to the ship as* BILLY *appears.)*

BILLY: Dad! Mom!

(BILLY *runs to them. They have a three-way embrace.*)

MICHAEL: Are you all right?

BILLY: I'm fine.

PRISCILLA: Don't let me go. Are you all right?
Talk to me.

BILLY: I'm fine.

PRISCILLA: Did they hurt you?

BILLY: No. But those math tests were really hard.

MICHAEL: How did you do?

BILLY: I aced 'em.

MICHAEL: That's my boy!

(*The lights flash and swirl for a moment, then stop.*)

(MICHAEL *draws* BILLY *to him.* PRISCILLA *knowingly
retreats.*)

MICHAEL: Listen, we've only got a second. There's been
a...a kind of a change in plans. I'm not staying here with
you.

BILLY: What do you mean?

MICHAEL: You see, they left one of their own. He's
taking my place on earth....

BILLY: ...and you're taking his place on the ship.

MICHAEL: Billy, I just...can you understand? I want it to
be clear—we won't ever see each other again.

BILLY: Wow—that is kind of a drag.

MICHAEL: It's a really huge drag.

(*They embrace.*)

BILLY: But Dad—wait a second! Once you get inside,
they'll give you this doohickey. It goes right here in

your tooth. *(He indicates.)* People send you their thoughts, and you can send yours too!

MICHAEL: You got a two-way?

BILLY: Oh yeah—if they like you, they make it a two-way.

(In the background, THE ALIEN *reacts.)*

BILLY: So when you get yours and I have mine, we can always be in contact with each other—anytime we want, just by thinking!

MICHAEL: Wow.

BILLY: Yeah, cool—huh?

MICHAEL: But Billy, can you understand why I have to do this?

BILLY: Oh yeah.

MICHAEL: You can.

BILLY: It's just like on this one Star Trek. These two guys were in the wrong universes from the beginning, and they had to get back to the universe they belonged in, even if that wasn't where they came from. Because the other universe was, like, where they belonged.

MICHAEL: That's right. That's it.

BILLY: You see? You always said Star Trek was crap, but sometimes it's just like life.

(Lights swirl and flash again, this time they don't stop.)

MICHAEL: I love you. *(He grabs* BILLY *and draws him close.)*

BILLY: I love you too, Dad. You better get going.

MICHAEL: I'm really going to miss you, Billy. I'll miss you a whole planet's worth.

BILLY: Me too, Dad.

(They embrace once more then pull away. BILLY starts to exit.)

MICHAEL: Mind your mother. Unless you really think she's wrong. In which case, try to make the ethical choice.

BILLY: 'kay, I will!

(BILLY crosses to PRISCILLA. The lights flash, whirl, become blinding as MICHAEL disappears into them.)

(THE ALIEN emerges from behind the log and takes his place at PRISCILLA's side.)

ALIEN: Hello.

BILLY: Hi.

ALIEN: I'm in love with your mother.

PRISCILLA: I hope that's all right.

BILLY: It's okay by me.

PRISCILLA: Really? You don't mind?

BILLY: He's got to be better than Ray, that's for sure.
   Besides, from what they said about him on the ship— *(To THE ALIEN)* —you sound great.

(They do a "special" handshake. Spaceships lights and noises off stage as it starts to rise. They all look towards it.)

(Softly, in the background, we hear music rising....)

(RAY and THE SHERIFF enter at a run. RAY still has his beer with him. They stop, awestruck at the rising ship.)

SHERIFF: Michael!... Billy!... Michael...

RAY: ...dang!

BILLY: Hey, do you hear that?

PRISCILLA: What the heck is that?

(The music rises now. It's Beethoven's Seventh Symphony, *end of the First Movement.)*

ALIEN & BILLY: Beethoven!

PRISCILLA: It's your father. It's his sign!

BILLY: They sure looove their Beethoven.

ALIEN: There he goes!

(Their heads slowly turn upwards to follow the ship over their heads, until they end up facing out to the audience. The music rises to a crescendo.)

SHERIFF: I told him to think about relocating, but holy cripes!

PRISCILLA: Good bye Michael!

BILLY: Good bye Dad!

RAY: And don't come crawlin' back, either!

ALIEN: Bye bye! Bye bye!

EVERYONE: *(But* RAY*)* Good bye! Good bye!

(Their hands reach out towards the audience to wave good bye as the music climaxes and the lights fade to black.)

END OF PLAY

www.ingramcontent.com/pod-product-compliance
Lightning Source LLC
Chambersburg PA
CBHW052203090426
42741CB00010B/2395